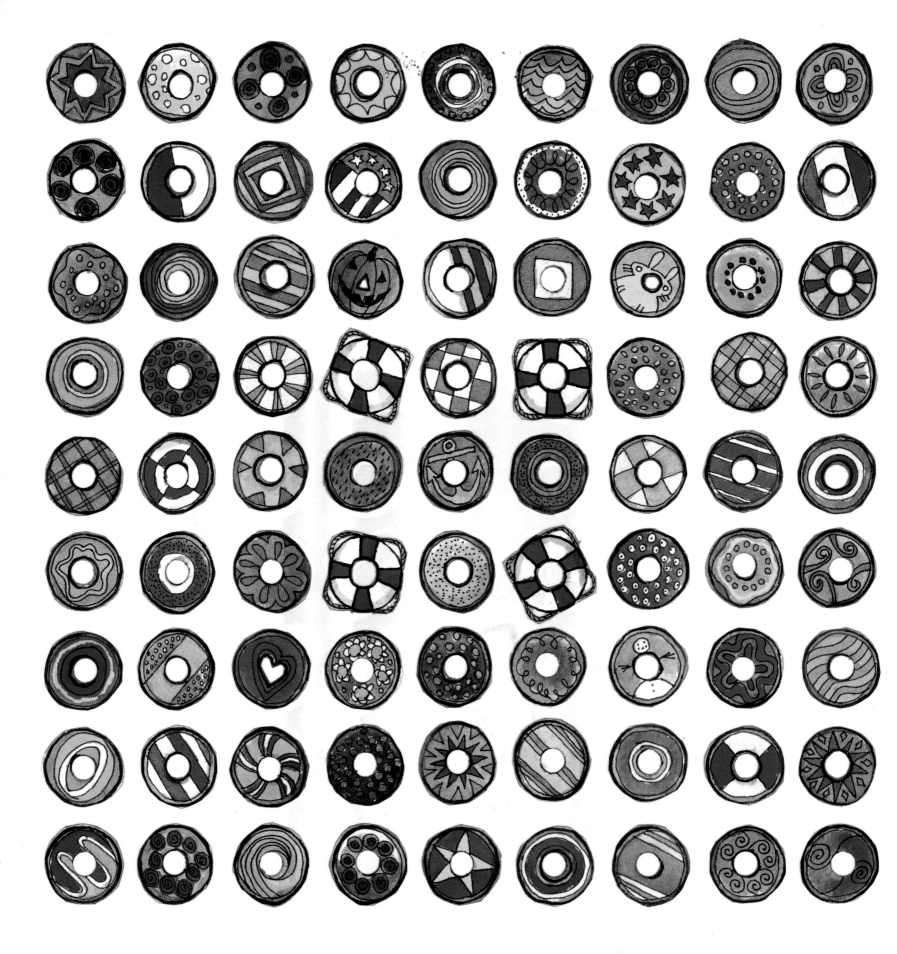

THE HOLE STORY OF THE DOUGHNUT

Pat Miller

illustrated by
Vincent X. Kirsch

HOUGHTON MIFFLIN HARCOURT
BOSTON   NEW YORK

For my favorite doughnut lovers:
Darcy, Madeleine, Wyatt, Walt, Colette, and Ada.
—P. M.

To Mona, who wishes that doughnuts did not have holes
so there would be more doughnut to eat.
—V. X. K.

Text copyright © 2016 by Pat Miller
Illustrations copyright © 2016 by Vincent X. Kirsch

www.hmhco.com

The text of this book is set in Cooper Old Style URW.

The illustrations were made with watercolor, black gesso, glue and cut hot press watercolor paper.

Photograph of Captain Gregory from the collections of the Camden Public Library.

Library of Congress Cataloging-in-Publication Data is on file.

ISBN 978-0-544-31961-5

Manufactured in China

SCP 10 9 8 7 6 5 4 3 2 1

4500574800

Few remember the master mariner Hanson Crockett Gregory, though he was bold and brave and bright.

But the pastry he invented more than 166 years ago is eaten daily by doughnut lovers everywhere. *This is his story.*

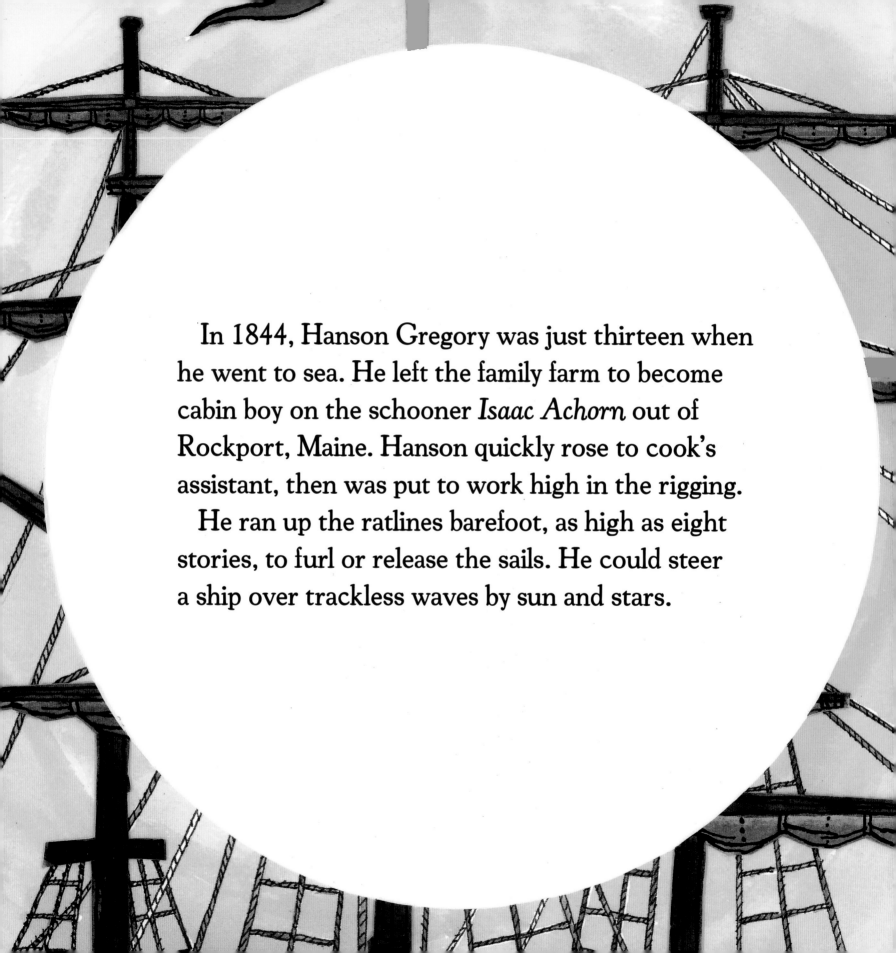

In 1844, Hanson Gregory was just thirteen when he went to sea. He left the family farm to become cabin boy on the schooner *Isaac Achorn* out of Rockport, Maine. Hanson quickly rose to cook's assistant, then was put to work high in the rigging.

He ran up the ratlines barefoot, as high as eight stories, to furl or release the sails. He could steer a ship over trackless waves by sun and stars.

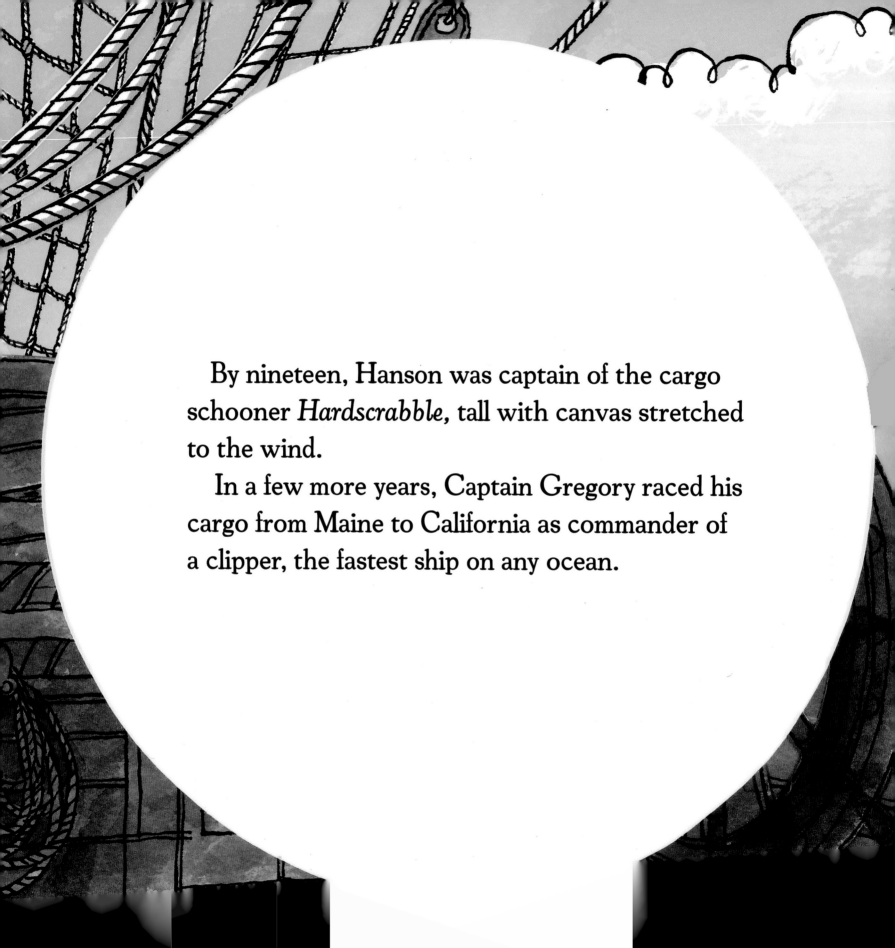

By nineteen, Hanson was captain of the cargo schooner *Hardscrabble*, tall with canvas stretched to the wind.

In a few more years, Captain Gregory raced his cargo from Maine to California as commander of a clipper, the fastest ship on any ocean.

On one voyage, he risked ship and crew to rescue seven Spanish sailors from certain death in a frigid sea. When the news reached Spain, Queen Isabella II awarded Captain Gregory a medal for heroism.

But what about the pastry?

For that, we have to go back to June 22, 1847.

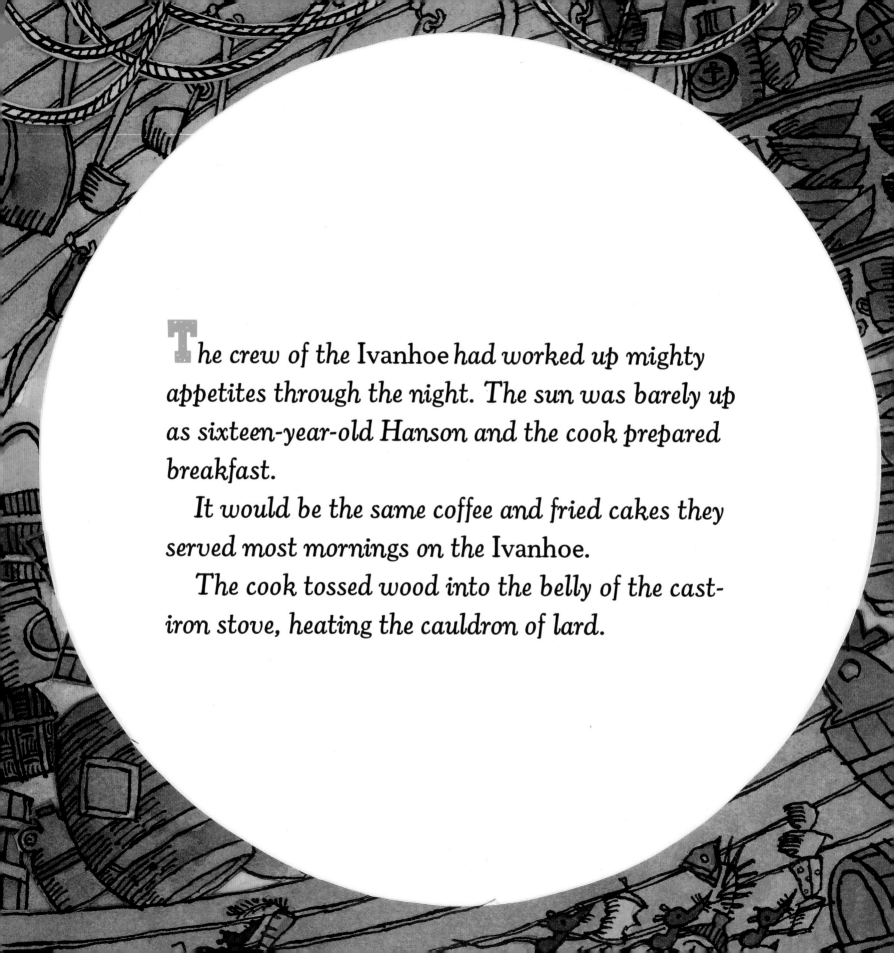

The crew of the Ivanhoe had worked up mighty appetites through the night. The sun was barely up as sixteen-year-old Hanson and the cook prepared breakfast.

It would be the same coffee and fried cakes they served most mornings on the Ivanhoe.

The cook tossed wood into the belly of the cast-iron stove, heating the cauldron of lard.

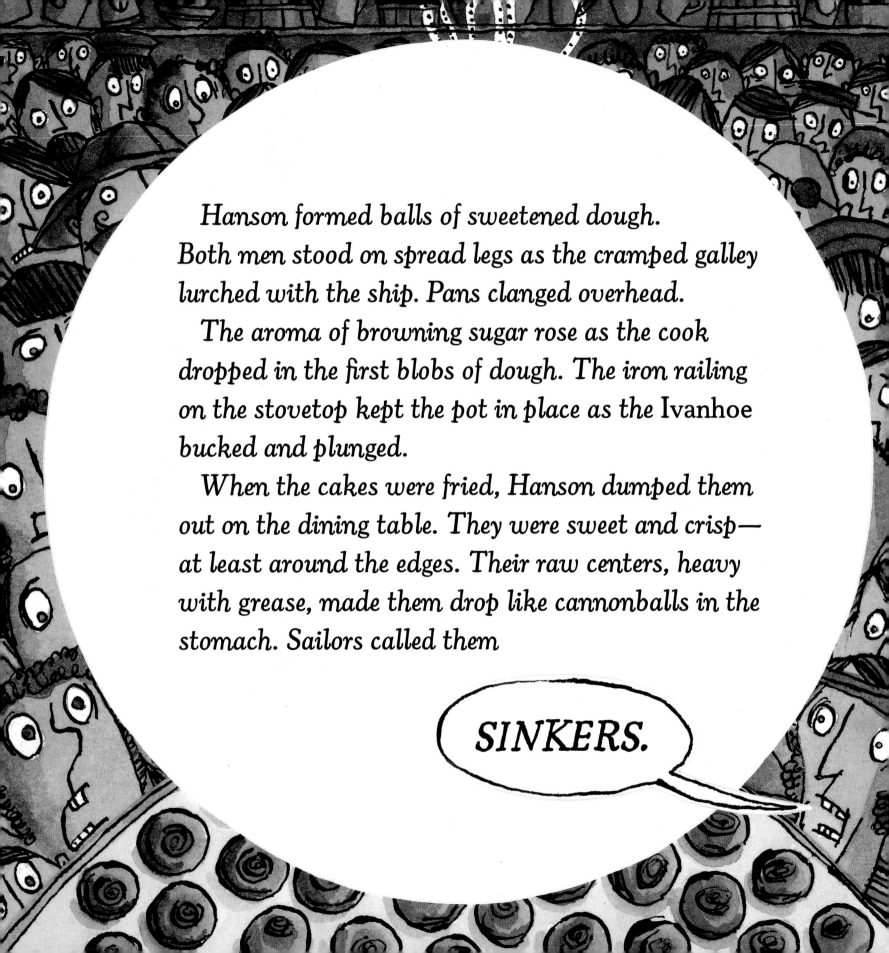

Hanson formed balls of sweetened dough. Both men stood on spread legs as the cramped galley lurched with the ship. Pans clanged overhead.

The aroma of browning sugar rose as the cook dropped in the first blobs of dough. The iron railing on the stovetop kept the pot in place as the Ivanhoe bucked and plunged.

When the cakes were fried, Hanson dumped them out on the dining table. They were sweet and crisp— at least around the edges. Their raw centers, heavy with grease, made them drop like cannonballs in the stomach. Sailors called them

SINKERS.

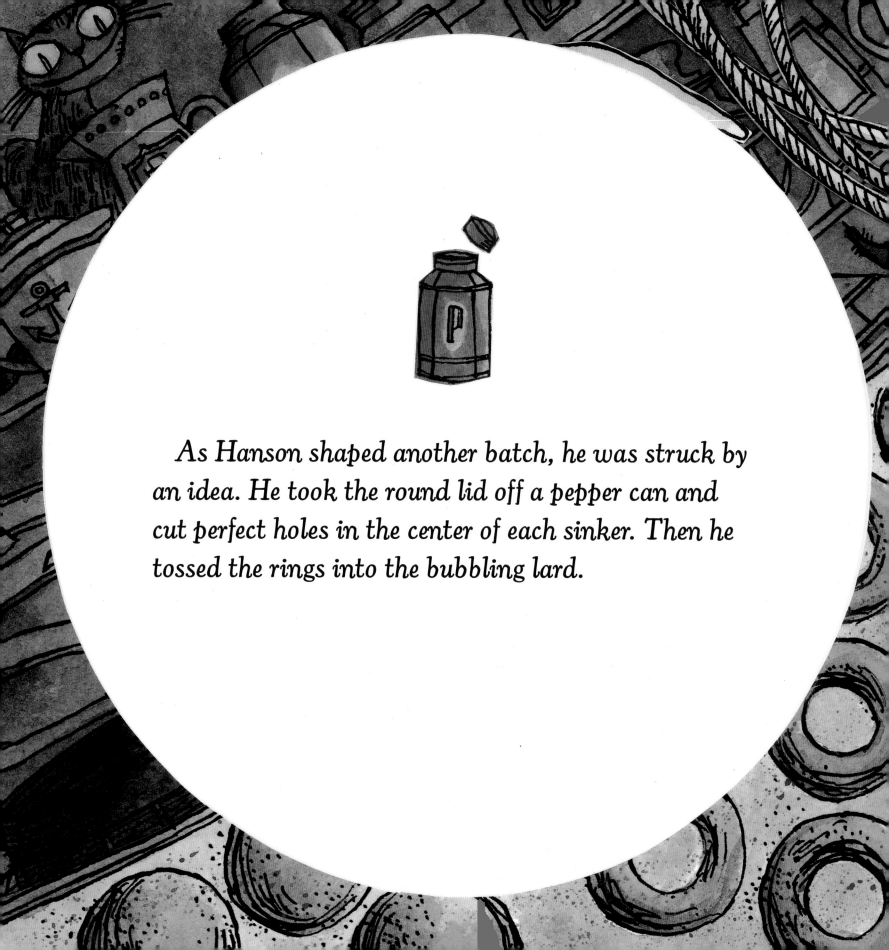

As Hanson shaped another batch, he was struck by an idea. He took the round lid off a pepper can and cut perfect holes in the center of each sinker. Then he tossed the rings into the bubbling lard.

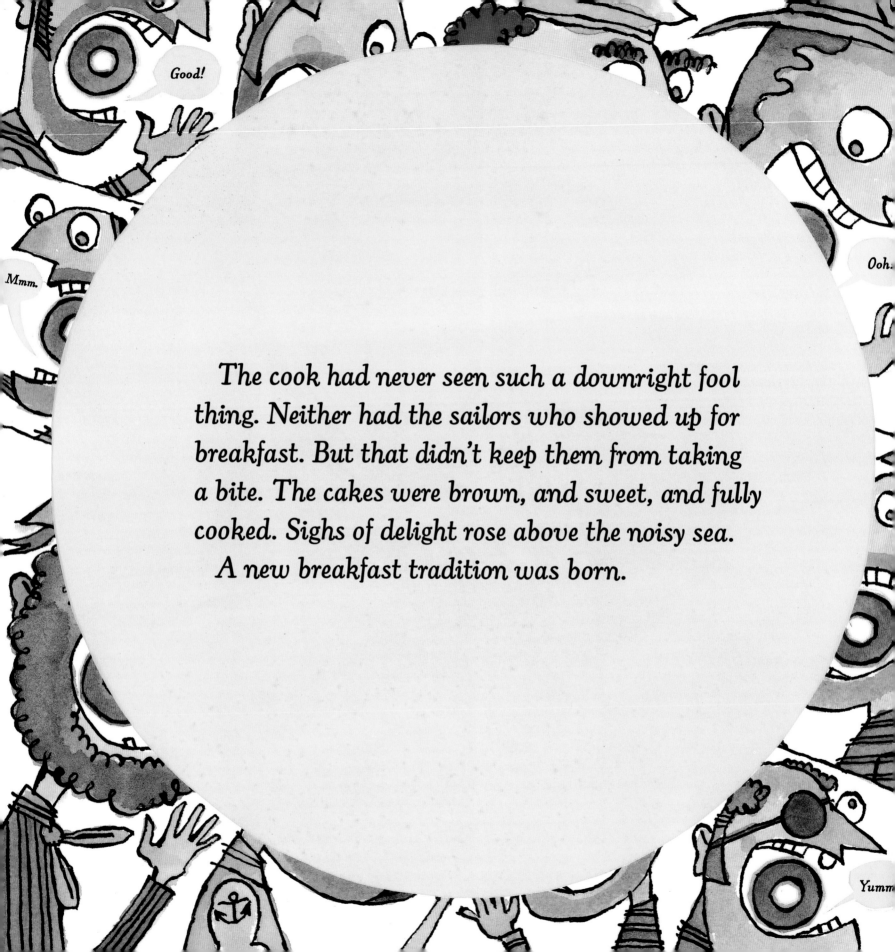

The cook had never seen such a downright fool thing. Neither had the sailors who showed up for breakfast. But that didn't keep them from taking a bite. The cakes were brown, and sweet, and fully cooked. Sighs of delight rose above the noisy sea.

A new breakfast tradition was born.

The teenage Hanson shared his invention with his mother. She cooked up large batches to sell in a friend's store, and on the docks to hungry sailors. Ships' cooks now served "holey cakes."

That's how
Hanson's invention
spread around
the world . . .

. . . and down the years and right into your stomach.

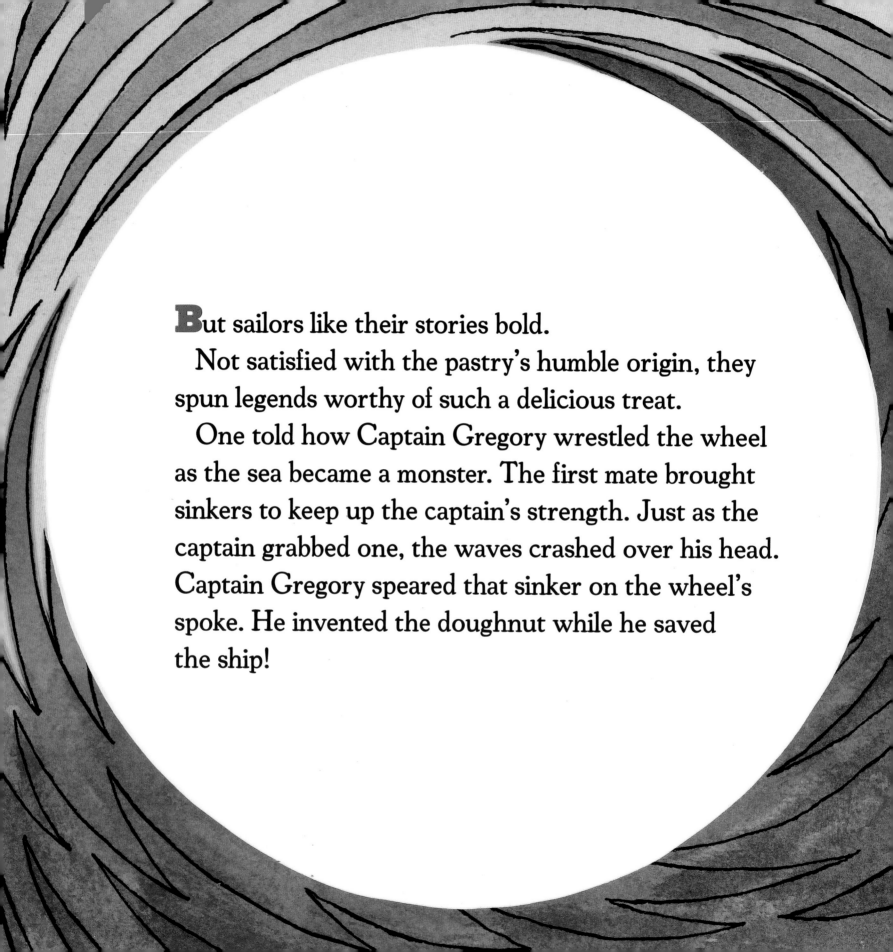

But sailors like their stories bold.

Not satisfied with the pastry's humble origin, they spun legends worthy of such a delicious treat.

One told how Captain Gregory wrestled the wheel as the sea became a monster. The first mate brought sinkers to keep up the captain's strength. Just as the captain grabbed one, the waves crashed over his head. Captain Gregory speared that sinker on the wheel's spoke. He invented the doughnut while he saved the ship!

Another legend tells how wild waves grabbed five
sailors and pulled them overboard right after breakfast.
With bellies full of oily pastries, they sank like stones.
Captain Gregory shouted, "Never again!" He used
a wooden belaying pin to punch holes in every cake
so they resembled the ship's life rings.

No sailor has since been drowned by his breakfast.

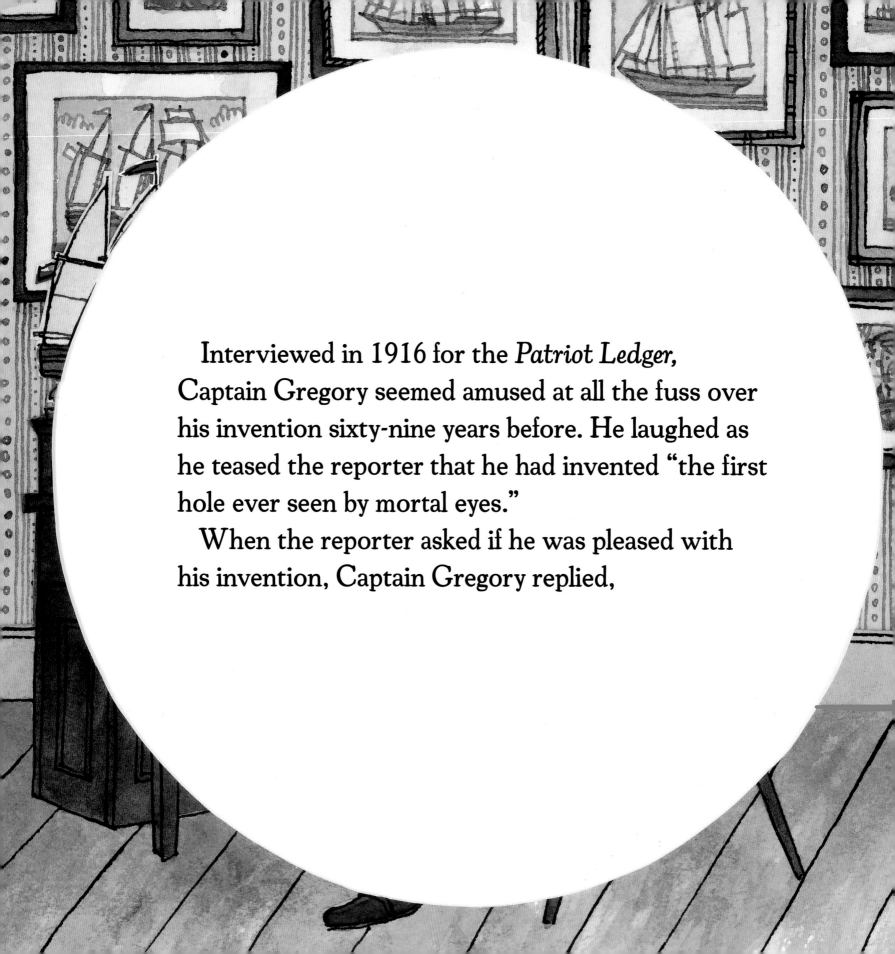

Interviewed in 1916 for the *Patriot Ledger,*
Captain Gregory seemed amused at all the fuss over
his invention sixty-nine years before. He laughed as
he teased the reporter that he had invented "the first
hole ever seen by mortal eyes."

When the reporter asked if he was pleased with
his invention, Captain Gregory replied,

At eighty-nine, Captain Gregory died
at the Sailors' Snug Harbor, a home for
sailors near Quincy, Massachusetts.

He was buried overlooking the sea where stormy weather can be spotted as readily as it once was from the quarterdeck of the *Hardscrabble*.

Whether you prefer chocolate or sprinkled, glazed or filled, raise your next tasty doughnut to the master mariner from Maine.

AUTHOR'S NOTE

Captain Gregory retired from the quarterdeck in 1868 at the age of thirty-six, forced from his beloved schooner by faster steam-powered ships. He became a mining engineer in the lime mines of Rockland, Maine.

Captain Gregory and wife, Mary Ann (Merrifield), had five daughters.

Since 1938, the first Friday in June has been designated National Doughnut Day to honor Helen Purviance and the women from the Salvation Army who made doughnuts near the battlefields during World War I.

In 1941, Henry Ellis challenged Captain Gregory's claim, saying the doughnut hole was created by his grandmother. Gregory was defended by his cousin's son, Fred E. Crockett. The Great Doughnut Debate, held at the Astoria Hotel in New York City, was judged by the author Clifton Fadiman and the gossip columnist Elsa Maxwell, among others. They agreed with Captain Gregory's claim. Ellis later admitted it was a publicity stunt on his part.

Hanson Crockett Gregory was honored in 1948 by the American Baker's Association as the inventor of the hole in the doughnut.

In the mid-1950s, Captain Gregory's headstone disappeared, leaving his grave unmarked for twenty years. In 1979, a teacher/historian named Harold Crowley located the gravesite. When Richard Hart, vice president of Dunkin Donuts, read the newspaper article about Gregory's missing grave marker, he announced that his company would pay for a new one.

On June 11, 1982, sixty-one years after the captain's death, area dignitaries dedicated his new headstone. Students from Snug Harbor Elementary gave speeches, sang songs, and ate doughnuts.

# TIMELINE

1831 Hanson Crockett Gregory is born to Hanson Phillip and Mary Ann (Barrows) Gregory in Clam Cove / Rockport, Maine, on November 20.

1844 Hanson serves aboard the *Isaac Achorn* at age thirteen.

1847 As cook's assistant on the *Ivanhoe,* Hanson invents the doughnut hole.

1853 On November 8, Hanson marries Mary Ann Merrifield in Camden.

1853-63 Hanson Gregory is captain and part owner of the schooner *Hardscrabble*.

1863 He registers for the Union draft.

1866-68 Captain Gregory makes his last voyage.

1915 On September 30, he is admitted to Sailors' Snug Harbor, a retirement home.

1916 Gregory is interviewed by the *Patriot Ledger* on March 20.

1921 On June 13, Hanson Crockett Gregory dies in Quincy, Massachusetts, at age eighty-nine.

1941 The Great Doughnut Debate validates Captain Gregory's claim to inventing the doughnut's hole. Astoria Hotel, New York City.

1947 A plaque is erected at Gregory's birthplace in Clam Cove, Maine.

1948 Hanson Crockett Gregory is honored by the American Bakers Association as the inventor of the hole in the doughnut.

1950 Open Kettle, begun in 1948, is renamed Dunkin Donuts in Quincy, Massachusetts.

1982 On June 11, children of the local school hold a ceremony to mark Gregory's gravesite. Dunkin Donuts provides the prominent headstone.

ACKNOWLEDGMENTS

I am grateful to the following individuals for answering my many questions and supplying copies of primary documents:

Theresa Tangney and Diane Costagliola, Reference Department, Thomas Crane Public Library, Quincy, Massachusetts.

Warren Riess, research associate professor, History and Marine Sciences, University of Maine, Walpole, Maine.

Kevin Johnson, photo archivist, Penobscot Marine Museum, Searsport, Maine.

Sandy Whiteley, librarian, Maine Maritime Museum, Bath, Maine.

Heather Moran, director, Walsh History Center, Camden Public Library, Camden, Maine.

Pat Schaefer, Collections Access and Research, the Museum of America and the Sea, Mystic Seaport, Connecticut.

Eric Pena, research volunteer, Stephen Phillips Memorial Library, Penobscot Marine Museum, Searsport, Maine.

SELECTED BIBLIOGRAPHY

Blackington, Alton. "Crisis Near in Battle of the Doughnut-Hole." *Boston Herald*, October 26, 1941, section B, p. 2.

Dyer, Barbara F. *Remembering Camden: Stories from an Old Maine Harbor*. Charleston, S.C.: History Press, 2007.

Eaton, Cyrus. *History of Thomaston, Rockland, and South Thomaston, Maine*, Vol. 2. Hallowell, Maine: Masters, Smith & Company, Printers, 1865.

Find a Grave (www.findagrave.com; accessed August 26, 2014).

"Invented the Doughnut Hole: Capt. Hanson Gregory of Sailors Snug Harbor Claims That Distinction." *Patriot Ledger*, March 20, 1916.

Mullins, Paul R. *Glazed America*. Gainesville: University Press of Florida, 2008.

O'Donnell, Bernie. "Doughnut's Inventor to Get Gravestone at Snug Harbor Cemetery." *Quincy Sun*, August 30, 1979.

"Official Recognition Finally Comes to Doughnut Inventor Buried Here." *Patriot Ledger*, November 1, 1947.

Shore Village Historical Society. *Around Rockland*. Rockland, Maine: Arcadia Publishing, 1996.

"Special Gravestone Honors Sailor Who Created a 'Hole' New Idea." *Patriot Ledger*, June 11, 1982.

Steinbert, Sally Levitt. *The Doughnut Book: The Whole Story in Words, Pictures and Outrageous Tales*. North Adams, Mass.: Storey Publishing, 2004.

"The Story of the Doughnut." Social Studies for Kids (www.socialstudiesforkids.com/articles/ushistory/doughnut_history.htm; accessed August 26, 2014).

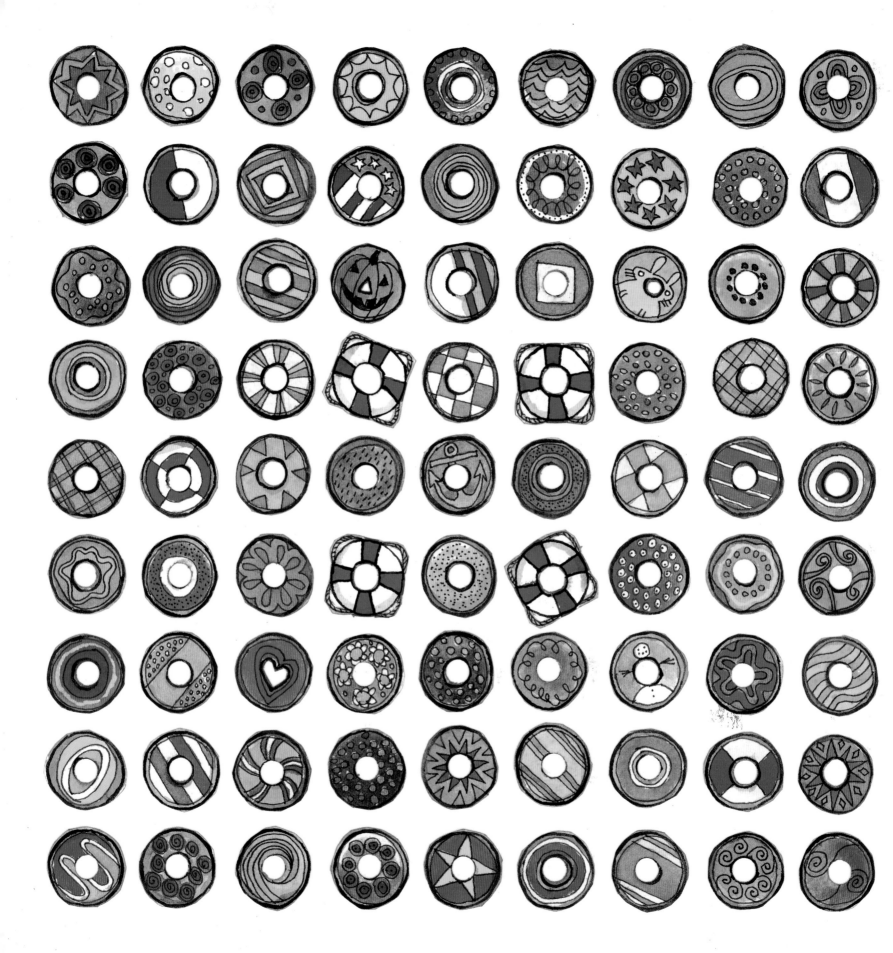